To my daughter, Maya

GORGONI

RIZZOLI
NEW YORK

BEYOND THE CANVAS

Artists of the Seventies and Eighties
Photographs and text by Gianfranco Gorgoni
Introduction by Leo Castelli

First published in the United States of America in 1985 by
RIZZOLI INTERNATIONAL PUBLICATIONS, INC.
597 Fifth Avenue, New York NY 10017

Library of Congress Cataloging-in-Publication Data

Gorgoni, Gianfranco.
    Beyond the canvas, artists of the seventies and eighties.

    1. Artists—Portraits. 2. Art, Modern—20th century.
I. Castelli, Leo. II. Title.
N7592.6.G67 1985   770'.92'4   85-43057
ISBN 0-8478-0662-6

Designed by Massimo Vignelli
Set in type by Typogram, New York City
Printed and bound in Japan

On the title page: *Michael Heizer, Mormon Mesa, Nevada,
1970;* on pages 6–7, *Leo Castelli and James Rosenquist,
Leo Castelli Gallery, New York, 1981*

Contents

Introduction

Leo Castelli

According to Gustave Flaubert, a work of art must always be considered independently from the private life of the artist. Certainly any product of creative effort—whatever you do, whatever I do, whatever the artist does—has a life of its own. Still, since the time of Vasari, the public has been fascinated by the lives of artists. Knowing about an artist's life-style helps us to understand his work to some extent, but even more important, it helps us to realize that the person who accomplishes these great things is a human being, with human concerns and problems. In other words, the artist is as separate from his work as his work is from him. By observing artists at home and at work, we learn about the process, rather than the products, of creativity.

The photographer is a privileged member of the public, and a talented photographer like Gianfranco Gorgoni can play an important role in revealing this human side of the artist. Many artists consider the photographer an intruder, and the photographic session a chore, even an ordeal. Naturally, when the subject is uncomfortable, the results suffer: instead of exposing humanness, the portrait invites an awe and respect for the artist that should rightly be directed toward his work. Gianfranco has succeeded in relaxing the artists whose portraits he takes by getting to know them. His interest is sincere; he has enjoyed his encounters with artists, he says, because they are the first to grasp and express truths about life. He has visited artists' studios and summer homes. He has attended their openings and installations. He has accompanied them on trips in cars, boats, trains, airplanes, and helicopters. He has gone out drinking with them and visited their families and seen movies with them. In short, he has shared parts of their lives.

The result of this method is that Gianfranco's photographs possess a unique quality of intimacy and veracity. It is almost as if he has a radar for an artist's creative frequency, a talent for judging—even provoking—the precise moment when an artist is at his or her best. For the Minimal artists, Gianfranco's expert skills are particularly important. His photographs are sometimes the only visual record of their works of art.

Gianfranco first came to my gallery in 1969, seeking advice about how to meet young and upcoming artists. His interest in new art movements had led to an assignment for the Italian magazine *L'Espresso,* and he wanted to photograph as many artists as he could. I was able to put him in touch with the ones that I knew, and a few weeks later he had the photographs that he needed.

In the meantime I had always wondered who might become the successor to Ugo Mulas, the great Italian photographer who had made a series of artists' portraits in the 1950s and 1960s. The photographs appeared in the book *New York: The New Art Scene* (1967) by Alan Solomon. What Ugo had done was extraordinary, but since that time no other photographer had come forward with the same talent and dedication to carry on what he had begun. Alan Solomon had decided to write a sequel to *New York,* and I suggested that Gianfranco would make the ideal collaborator. I have a vivid recollection of the tragic day in February 1970, when Gianfranco went to discuss the book at Alan's home, where Alan was convalescing from a heart ailment. That day, while he and Gianfranco laid out the plans for their project, Alan died of a heart attack—almost in Gianfranco's arms. Since I had brought Alan and Gianfranco together, I felt somewhat responsible, and I made a selection of artists for the book, with Gianfranco and the new author Grégoire Müller. *The New Avant-Garde: Issues for the Art of the Seventies* appeared in 1972, and Gianfranco's photographs were widely acclaimed.

In a sense, *Beyond the Canvas* is the sequel to the *New Avant-Garde,* except that it is even more Gianfranco's book and shows the whole range of his continuing work with artists. When he came to the United States in 1968 on his first visit to this country, it was specifically to document artists in the tradition of Mulas, whose book he admired. He had been a commercial and fashion photographer in Milan, and he intended to return to Italy in a few months. Instead he remained in New York as a permanent resident, not returning to his homeland until three years later, to make photographs for the *New Avant-Garde.* In the past seventeen years, whether or not he has had a specific assignment, Gianfranco has continued to build an impressive archive of artists' pictures, only partly represented by those in this book. Even when he has journalistic assignments for *Fortune, GEO, Time,* and other major magazines, he makes time for artists, many of whom now call upon him.

My own involvement with American and European artists has spanned more than three decades, and I have known many of the artists portrayed in Gianfranco's photographs—either in person or through their work. In the beginning I often idolized artists, but I also realized that they did not want excessive admiration, only the everyday kind of conversation that anyone else needs. Over the years many artists have become true friends.

After World War II, when I had just moved to the United States and before I had opened a gallery, I admired the Abstract Expressionists, particularly Jackson Pollock and

Willem de Kooning. Pollock, who died before Gianfranco came to New York, was one hundred percent American; de Kooning's European roots were always there; but as artists I considered them equally great. Pollock could be sweet and interesting when he was in a good mood, but turned violent when he had been drinking too much. De Kooning was sociable and friendly, and I came to know him well in the late 1940s, when he and Elaine de Kooning stayed with me and Ileana (my wife at that time, now Ileana Sonnabend) at our house in East Hampton, Long Island. I see him seldom now, and I have heard that his mind wanders. Nevertheless his painting is better than ever, so art must come from deep unconscious sources.

During those days I was involved with a group of artists who shared their work and ideas by meeting in informal gatherings at a place called the Club and at the Cedar Street Tavern. Since museums then paid little attention to contemporary American painting (even the Museum of Modern Art showed mainly European artists), we decided to correct this imbalance by mounting our own show in the spring of 1951. We rented two floors of a building scheduled for demolition, fixed them up, and announced the opening of the Ninth Street Show. De Kooning, Franz Kline, and Marca-Relli, among others, participated in the organization, and we invited several younger artists, of whom the youngest was Robert Rauschenberg. I had seen Rauschenberg's first show at the Betty Parsons Gallery earlier that year and had asked him to contribute.

I opened my first gallery in the United States at 4 East Seventy-seventh Street in 1957, and Rauschenberg was one of my first candidates. The variety of his production since then has been simply amazing. He has worked with paper at the world's oldest paper mill in China; he has produced ceramics— some of monumental size using classical imagery of all periods—in Japan; and he has created paintings a quarter of a mile long. His imagination has no limits, and at the age of fifty-nine he is still as spritely and as enthusiastic about his projects as he was thirty years ago. Now he is involved in a traveling exhibition of his work that will last five years and visit twenty-two countries. As the exhibition continues it will grow in scope, as Rauschenberg adds a painting inspired by each country. The tour will culminate in Washington, D.C., at the National Gallery of Art.

Through Rauschenberg I met Jasper Johns. I experienced a *coup de foudre* when I saw Johns's work for the first time, at *Artists of the New York School: Second Generation,* an exhibition organized by Meyer Schapiro in 1957 at the Jewish Museum. I knew all of the other painters in the exhibition, but Johns's green target painting came as a complete surprise. A

few days later I met Johns quite by accident when I was visiting Rauschenberg's studio; it turned out that Johns occupied the studio below.

Johns is as uncommunicative about his feelings (at least verbally) as Rauschenberg is open, but his exquisite courtesy is that of a Southern gentleman of days past. He can, however, be waspish when something goes against his grain. He is a splendid host, and his cuisine is of the highest quality. He is generally serious, but can laugh heartily when something strikes him as amusing. We know about philosopher-kings. Jasper is a philosopher-painter, if there ever was one.

Following these two artists, who were the foundation of my gallery, my greatest discovery was Frank Stella. A critic, perhaps Robert Rosenblum, told me about a young painter who had just graduated from Princeton University. In September 1959 I went to Stella's studio on West Broadway, in the part of town now called SoHo, where I saw for the first time his remarkable black paintings. I decided immediately that I must have them in my gallery. At about the same time Dorothy Miller, assistant to Alfred H. Barr, then the Director of Museum Collections at the Museum of Modern Art, was looking for young artists to include in her *16 Americans* exhibition. Rauschenberg, Johns, and Ellsworth Kelly had already been selected. I told her about the young artist whose work I had just seen, and together we visited Stella's studio. She said nothing in front of Stella, but afterwards, down on the street, she said excitedly, "I *must* have that artist in my show." I told her I thought it was absurd that an artist who had hardly shown at all (Stella had been included in a group show at the Tibor de Nagy Gallery the previous spring) should be catapulted into a major museum exhibition. I also admitted that it was disturbing to my own plans to show him that fall. She said never mind, she had to have him, and I gave in. So Frank Stella began his career at the Museum of Modern Art. Today that dramatic beginning has been justified by Stella's endless innovation. His studio in an old theater on Thirteenth Street is truly a factory of invention.

In Paris at the end of the 1950s, I met the Bulgarian artist Christo for the first time. He had blocked a narrow street with a wall of oil drums in various colors—a marvelous work that was way ahead of its time. Then he came to America and we became good friends. He had one show at the gallery—a storefront installation—but the sort of works he wanted to produce could not be contained in a gallery. The person who was able to make his dreams a reality was his wife, Jeanne-Claude. The daughter of a French general, Jeanne-Claude inherited her father's ability to orchestrate grand projects and marshal troops. She is the organizer who stages the environmental events—the wrappings of buildings and coastlines, the curtains, the *Running Fence*—that Christo originates, which have become more ambitious over the years.

For me the artist to signal the new direction the 1960s would take was Roy Lichtenstein. He appeared at the gallery in 1961 with some canvases under his arm. These were the paintings based on comic strips and other commercial images, including the famous girl with a beach ball, purchased by Philip Johnson and given by him to the Museum of Modern Art. They were outrageous, but of course since I was used to Rauschenberg's and Johns's audacities, they did not seem so outrageous to me. And I was not the only one to admire them. Marcel Duchamp was alive at the time, and when he saw Lichtenstein's work in 1962, he approved of it. Rauschenberg was a bit taken aback when I showed him Roy's work, but the next day he said he had thought it over, and agreed that it was very good. It took Jasper Johns a little longer to accept Lichtenstein, but in the end he did.

With Andy Warhol I was slower to react. I encountered his work in the early 1960s, about the same time I discovered Lichtenstein's. It at first seemed to me that what Warhol was doing, with his comic strips and consumer goods, was very similar to what Lichtenstein was after, and I did not want to have two similar artists in the gallery. Little did I know that both artists were part of an important movement, that a few months later would be called Pop Art. Warhol told me that I was wrong to identify his work so closely with Lichtenstein's, and he soon proved it. At his first exhibition at Eleanor Ward's Stable Gallery (it was named after a real stable that was the first home of the gallery and that even after many years always smelled of horses), he showed the multiple Marilyn Monroe and Elvis Presley pictures, and the Brillo boxes. He joined me in 1964, and we showed his beautiful pictures of flowers of all sizes and colors. One of the most exciting shows ever mounted at the Seventy-seventh Street gallery was Warhol's silkscreened prints of a pink cow, with which we wallpapered the whole back room. (It was easy enough to put up but awful to take down.) Warhol directly contradicts Flaubert's dictum that art and the artist must be separate. His life has been his art, and he is so public about his career that only people totally disinterested in art and media can have escaped hearing about him and seeing his work.

Another artist who came to my gallery in 1964 is James Rosenquist. He had been a billboard painter and then had begun his artistic career with Richard Bellamy's Green Gallery, but his ambition was to be in the same gallery with Rauschenberg, Johns, and Lichtenstein. His first show at the Castelli Gallery was the sensational *F-111* painting that went

all around the gallery walls. The collector Robert Scull bought it, and he made the purchase into a media event. It may have been an act of self-promotion, but the publicity served the artist—and the gallery—as well.

Rosenquist's life changed dramatically in 1971, when he was involved in a car accident in which his wife and son were badly hurt. For several years he was preoccupied with their recovery, and his work slowed down. In the past five years, though, he has produced some of his best paintings. Among them is a series, so far numbering three works, each measuring forty-six by eighteen feet.

Of the Pop artists in my gallery, Claes Oldenburg was the last to arrive. I admired him from the beginning of his career, when his theme was huge hamburgers, pies, and other plaster sculptures, but he decided, or so I heard, that he might be overshadowed by the other great artists in my gallery. Therefore, after the collapse of the Green Gallery in 1965, he joined Sidney Janis. Eventually, though, he came to me, and was responsible for one of the best shows ever installed at the gallery. He decided that *Crusoe's Umbrella,* a monumental sculpture that now sits in a plaza in Des Moines, Iowa, should be reproduced to actual size, as if intersected by the gallery ceiling and walls. Had it not been for ample explanatory materials, the show would have been utterly incomprehensible—just a roomful of enormous green shapes. For many years Oldenburg has primarily been involved in monumental commissions, such as the mouse in Newport, Rhode Island, which Gorgoni photographed; the lipstick at Yale University; and the baseball bat in Chicago. But his models and drawings continue to delight those of us who cannot travel to these sites.

During the period of Minimal and Conceptual Art that followed the Pop era, I exhibited the work of many new artists. Donald Judd was one of these. His work consists mostly of boxes in different media, such as steel, galvanized iron, anodized aluminum, plywood, and Plexiglas, featured singly or in the mathematical progression called the Fibonacci series. The boxes are designed to be hung on the wall or put on the floor. They have an extraordinary purity and yet are immensely, almost romantically, appealing to the eye.

Another artist I began to exhibit at this time was Robert Morris. He showed at the Green Gallery at first, and the last two shows he had there featured two very different kinds of pieces. At one of them he exhibited small Sculpmetal sculptures. I have several of these, a brain covered with dollar bills, for example, and a little piece of furniture with a fist on top of it and a gray glove in its drawer. The other show consisted entirely of Minimal pieces. When the Green Gallery closed, I asked Jasper Johns for advice. "Oh yes," he said, "you should definitely take him on. I saw a show of his recently and I really liked it." "Yes," I said, "but which one?" "Well, those Surrealist pieces." "Oh, that's not what struck me at all," I said. "I saw the Minimal pieces, and their spareness really impressed me." I did take Morris on, and he has been incredibly versatile, moving in those original two directions—the Surreal and the Minimal, sometimes combining influences of the two. In fact, he has done so many things in so many styles that people are stupefied by his somersaults.

Richard Serra is another sculptor whose work I began to show in the late 1960s. His early sculptures were made with large lead plates, but those, being soft, tended to collapse. He turned to steel, and erected his first large tower piece of four steel plates at the Stedelijk Museum in Amsterdam in 1975. The museum had earmarked a large sum of money for the installation, but it turned out that a few feet below the site, the ground turned to water. A special platform had to be built to support the piece, and that increased the expense by half of the original amount set aside. In the end neither Serra nor I made a penny on the transaction. Serra at least got a free trip to Amsterdam and lodging, and the museum paid my hotel bill, which was indeed a generous act, since I had made quite a few telephone calls to New York.

In 1985 Serra became the center of a controversy, when the General Services Administration concluded that his *Tilted Arc* sculpture could not be kept in the public space for which it had been commissioned because of the violent rejection of the piece by the people who worked in the buildings surrounding the plaza in which it stands. The conflict may go on for years, but in the meantime articles and television stories seem to appear every week. It has become a *cause célèbre* and ironically has made Serra into one of the best-known artists in the world today, second perhaps only to Andy Warhol in notoriety.

In the late 1960s I also took on Dan Flavin, who uses fluorescent tubes in various lengths and colors in environmental interiors. Then and now I have enjoyed both Flavin's work, which I find has an otherworldly beauty, and his company. He likes to eat and to drink well and is a connoisseur of good wines—so much so that when you go to a restaurant with him and he begins to consult the wine list, you get worried. His health does not permit him to enjoy these pleasures quite as much as he used to, but he is still a *bon vivant*.

Another artist to appear at this time was Bruce Nauman, an exceptionally original artist and a remarkable character.

Nauman is like Johns—a deep thinker, quiet and unassuming. Everything he touches is fresh and new. Words often feature in his works, incorporated, for example, in neon signs that flash on and off. Early in his career he made a series of wax-relief sculptures that were visual puns. I own one shaped like the back of a man's coat and tied with ropes, titled *Henry Moore Bound to Fail*. Among the other media that he uses is photography, in which his penchant for puns is especially evident. He has also made environmental pieces in which enclosed light plays an important role.

For a long time after the Minimalists and Conceptualists appeared, the art scene seemed quiet. Then almost out of the blue came painters who once again expressed themselves in paint on canvas: Georg Baselitz, Anselm Kiefer, Jörg Immendorff, A. R. Penck, and other younger artists, who followed Joseph Beuys and his contemporaries as the second wave of German artists after World War II. Italy produced the remarkable painters who go under the rubric of the Three Cs— Sandro Chia, Francesco Clemente, and Enzo Cucchi—along with Mimmo Paladino and Nicola de Maria.

I was a bit overwhelmed by this new development but realized that if I wanted to continue to be involved with the new, I would have to accept these movements. I demonstrated my commitment by having exhibitions of Julian Schnabel and David Salle, who had joined their Italian and German counterparts in this expressionist style, as well as of Chia and Clemente. Soon my first German painter, Georg-Jiri Dokoupil, and a Spanish artist, Miguel Barcelo, will join the roster.

Even newer than these artists are the graffiti painters, who began their careers literally on the streets, painting walls with distinctive, colorful images. The first one I noticed was Jean-Michel Basquiat, at one of those imaginative shows organized by Alanna Heiss at P. S. 1 in Long Island City. Then I noticed Keith Haring, whom I am planning to show in 1985 in conjunction with Tony Shafrazi. Haring seems the most intellectual of this group, and his paintings remind me of the work that Penck is doing right now. These new painters appeared first in the galleries of the East Village, today's proving ground for young artists.

There are of course many important artists with whose lives and work I am less familiar, from Georgia O'Keeffe, the oldest artist represented here, to Kenny Scharf, one of the youngest. All of them are part of the story of the art of our time. Thanks to Gianfranco Gorgoni, it is a story in pictures.

CARL ANDRE

Conceptual artists of the 1970s were especially hard to photograph at work, because their work was thinking, drawing, and talking. After Pop Art, which was like Disneyland, art got serious. The Conceptual artists not only talked more than other painters and sculptors, but they also tried to make a piece out of everything they said. Since most of them did not physically make their artworks once they had the idea and made the drawing, they idolized the real "workers" among artists of the past. Carl Andre, for example, always talked about Brancusi and his sculpture. Though I never photographed Andre creating one of his pieces in the physical sense, we once spent the day together roaming the Lower West Side taking photographs of objects that looked like his pieces—manhole covers and big metal plates and piles of bricks next to the curb.

Andre was against having his portrait taken, but after we had known each other for a little while, and I had made many photographs of his pieces, I ran into him on the street one day when I had my camera. "Don't worry," I told him. "We won't take a big picture, just a little one, like an identification picture." He said OK, but after just two shots he said no, no, no, and held up his hands. He wanted his work to represent him, not a picture of his face. But I had two shots, and one of them was pretty good.

Opposite page: *New York, 1970;* pages 14–15: *Solomon R. Guggenheim Museum, New York, 1970*

JOSEPH BEUYS

In 1971 I went to Düsseldorf to meet Joseph Beuys. I didn't know him, and I didn't know his work, but I arrived at the hotel and turned on the TV just in time to see the beginning of "Joseph Beuys and His Classroom." For some reason I had the camera ready, and I started to photograph the TV screen where Joseph Beuys was doing a performance, throwing water.

The next day I went to his studio. He could speak only German then, so we didn't talk much. He made me understand we should go to see an exhibition of his work, a few miles away, in Holland. We got into his car and drove along the autobahn. At one point I looked over and saw a swamp. Sometimes with artists you want to propose something, but you really don't dare, because they might react badly. But with Beuys I made him understand that we should stop because the swamp was so beautiful.

We got out of the car and birds started to fly overhead, big white water birds, and Beuys ran after them, flapping his arms. I could see him getting into the feeling of the swamp, so I asked, "Could we do something with water?" The next thing I knew he was going down into the swamp with his hat floating on it. He did a piece—unique—just for me. Then he got out, wrung himself out, and we got back into the car and went to the museum. Beuys walked right in, squish, squish, across the marble floor, and when the museum director came out Beuys gave him a big wet hug.

Several years later I had a studio at P.S. 1, the artist's space in Long Island City. I had made a print of a portrait I had made of Beuys in Germany, but it was a reject, so I had crumpled it up. The next day I found it and decided I liked it, so I pinned it up on the wall. One day Beuys came to P.S. 1 for a visit. I wasn't there, but my assistant saw him poke his head through the door. Beuys spotted his picture and said, "What a fantastic portrait—but didn't an Italian photographer make it?" Ciccio said, "Yes, Gianfranco." So Beuys signed the photograph, "With love to Gianfranco, Joseph Beuys."

Düsseldorf, West Germany, 1971

Eindhoven, Netherlands, 1971

Eindhoven, Netherlands, 1971; pages 20–21: *Eindhoven, Netherlands, 1971*

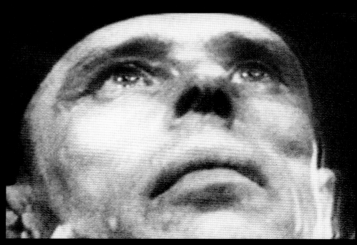

Düsseldorf, West Germany, 1971

Düsseldorf, West Germany, 1971

JONATHAN BOROFSKY

A few years ago when I was living in a loft over the Paula
Cooper Gallery, I came downstairs late at night and saw
the lights on: Jonathan Borofsky was installing a show.
I introduced myself, and he continued to work as I took
photographs. He used a light projector to cast silhouettes
and then painted them on the wall. He hardly said anything,
and it was very quiet. In the dark, with Borofsky moving
around and creating giant shadows, it was magical—more
like a dance performance than an artist's installation. I felt
privileged to be the only witness to so much intensity.

Opposite page: *Paula Cooper Gallery, New York, 1982*

Paula Cooper Gallery, New York, 1982

Paula Cooper Gallery, New York, 1982

Paula Cooper Gallery, New York, 1982

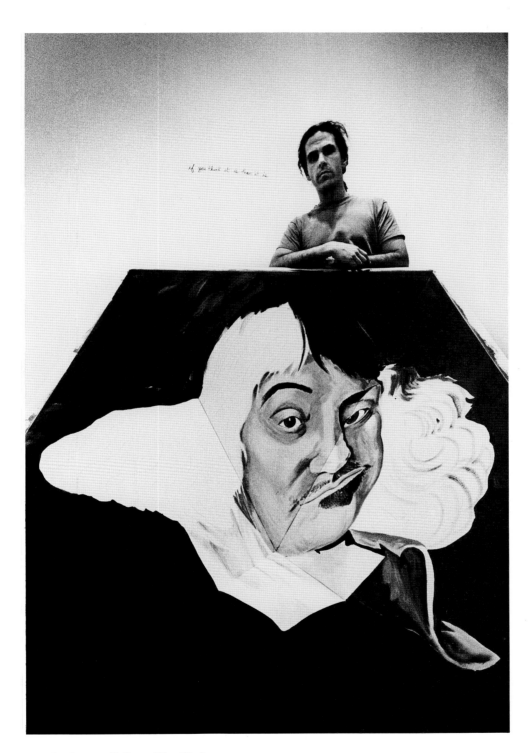

Paula Cooper Gallery, New York, 1982;
pages 30–31: *Paula Cooper Gallery,*
New York, 1982

SANDRO CHIA

The first time I met Sandro was in Italy. He was walking down the street with my *New Avant-Garde* under his arm, and I said, "You know, this is my book," and he said, "Oh, *you* are Gorgoni." This was 1972 or 1973. I wanted to do a project on Italian Conceptual artists, but for some reason I could never put them together. There was always some problem—no unity among the group. I knew Sandro and Francesco Clemente, but they were very young and I didn't think to photograph them.

A few years later I heard that Sandro was coming to New York. We met again, and I went to his studio and took a lot of pictures. We became friendly, and I visited him in the country. He likes to hunt in the wintertime, and I remember one time he shot a deer and we had venison for lunch. Of the Italian painters I have photographed, Sandro is the most at home in the United States and the most outgoing. Sandro has no problem having his picture taken.

Opposite page and pages 34–35, 38–39: *New York, 1983;* pages 36–37: *New York, 1984*

CHRISTO

Photographers always take part in Christo's projects, because that is one of the ways he presents his work. For a while he had two photographers working for him full-time. They did the *Valley Curtain*; they went to Australia. Then in 1974 or 1975 I met him and his wife, Jeanne-Claude, in the stairway of my building, and Jeanne-Claude said, "We want to talk to you about something." I went to see them the next week. They were preparing the *Running Fence*, and Christo explained that besides documenting the making of the piece they wanted portraits of the owners of the twenty-four miles of land that the piece would run through, so I agreed to work with them. I was the only photographer on that project, and it was a little scary because of its vast dimensions.

Christo is full of energy. He started early in the morning, helped the students who were setting up the fence, and went with me to do the photography. Even before work on the fence itself began, he was busy. It was incredible to see this long-haired Bulgarian trying to explain what he was going to do to California farmers who had never even been to San Francisco and knew very little about art.

Most of the time during the work I had a helicopter standing by, especially at dawn and dusk when the light changes so quickly. The piece changed character all of the time, depending on the wind conditions and the time of day. When Christo went with me I gave him my ideas as a photographer about what we could do with lenses and framing. As much as I learned from him as an artist, I also think he learned something from my stubbornness as a photographer.

Abu Dhabi, United Arab Emirates, 1981; pages 42–43: Running
Fence, *Marin-Sonoma Counties, California, 1976;* pages 44–45:
Newport, Rhode Island, 1974; pages 46–47: Surrounded
Islands, *Miami, 1983*

FRANCESCO CLEMENTE

When Francesco had just arrived in New York, he and his family came to my house for dinner. His baby had just been born, and we put her on the floor as we had dinner and started talking. We talked for a long time about what kind of projects we could do together, articles and so on, but after that evening we never got together again. Then several years later, I got an assignment from *GEO*, and everything we talked about that night came true.

Even before he moved to the United States Francesco spent a lot of time in Madras, India. I was able to visit him there once. We went to a cobra sanctuary next to his house, where seven or eight cobras live. In his studio he has a mynah bird flying around and incense burning. Seeing Francesco in India made me understand his painting.

New York, 1982

Madras, India, 1984

New York, 1983

New York, 1983

New York, 1983; pages 54–55: *With Alba Clemente,*
Mary Boone Gallery, New York, 1983

Madras, India, 1984; opposite page: *New York, 1984*

CHUCK CLOSE

Chuck Close works from photographs, and he often works in series, so when he held up the plastic sleeve that was on the table, I knew that would be his portrait—his face repeated many times as in his paintings.

Opposite page: *New York, 1973*

New York, 1973; opposite page: *New York, 1973*

ENZO CUCCHI

I met Sandro Chia in Italy and photographed him in New York.
I met Enzo Cucchi in New York and photographed him in
Italy. It is a funny coincidence, but it suits their personalities.
Sandro is very American. Enzo is very Italian. In Italy he lives
in a small town, and he needs all of the little pleasures and the
deep feeling that Italy gives him.

Since he has such a close connection to the Italian countryside,
I decided to photograph him in a few places that Italy is
known for—the Piazza Navona, the Via Appia Antica. The
cobblestones there reminded me of his paintings, particularly
since it was raining. We spent all day on the street and came
in soaked to the skin.

Opposite page: *Via Appia Antica, Rome, 1984;* pages 64–65: *Piazza
Navona, Rome, 1984;* pages 66–67: *Ancona, Italy, 1984*

WILLEM DE KOONING

Someone told me that Willem de Kooning lived in the
Hamptons on Long Island, so one time when I was out there, I
started walking around looking for his house. Finally I went
through a gate into a backyard and turned around and there he
was, behind a big plate-glass window, painting. I had found
his studio without realizing it. I knocked on the glass, and he
gestured for me to go to the door. "The phone is over there,"
he said. I told him I wasn't the repairman; I was an Italian
photographer taking pictures of artists. He apologized and
invited me in. Then he went back to painting, and I started
to wander around.

His studio is very large, almost like a boat, with a catwalk
around the edge. At one point I saw him looking around for me.
When he spotted me overhead he said, "This painting here—
doesn't it look like the Sistine Chapel?" I said I didn't know, it
looked pretty abstract to me. Then he said, "You see that group
of paintings over there? Some of them I have been working
on for ten years. I pick them up, they look like they're finished,
then I give them another look, and I start all over again."

Opposite page: *East Hampton, Long Island, 1972*

East Hampton, Long Island, 1972; opposite page and pages
72–73, 74–75: East Hampton, Long Island, 1972

WALTER DE MARIA

We met in a bar on Sunset Boulevard in Los Angeles. I had already made plans to go back to New York, but after we had been talking and drinking, he said he was going to the desert to work on a chalk piece, and he asked if I wanted to come along.

We landed in a dry lake in the middle of nowhere. De Maria worked all day with just a few tools on a big cross. From the ground it was impossible to tell what he was doing, so I went back up in the plane to take pictures. I was amazed: the lines of the cross, one about five hundred and the other about one thousand feet long, were absolutely straight.

Dry Lake, Nevada, 1970; pages 78–79: *Dry Lake, Nevada, 1970*

Dry Lake, Nevada, 1970; opposite page and pages 82–83:
Dry Lake, Nevada, 1970

MARK DI SUVERO

During the Vietnam War, Mark di Suvero left the United States in protest and went to live in Venice. That's where I met him, in 1973, when I went with Barbara Rose to work on an article about him. Unfortunately, right after we met, the three of us were walking down the street when a fellow came by who owed me money. I spoke to him, he insulted me, and I punched him in the face. So, right after he met me, di Suvero had to go with me to the police station. He always reminds me of it when I see him.

Di Suvero is someone I have photographed over a period of time, in many places—Italy, France, California. He is incredibly exuberant, and unlike many other artists during the 1970s, he was always very involved in the making of his work. He was seriously injured in an accident in 1960, but that didn't stop him from working on his large pieces. He not only did the intellectual preparation, but also cut the steel, welded the pieces together, shifted them with a crane, and climbed on top of them.

Opposite page: *Venice, Italy, 1973*

Chalon-sur-Saône, France, 1974

Venice, Italy, 1975

New York, 1975

New York, 1975

New York, 1975

New York, 1975; pages 92–93: *Chalon-sur-Saône, France, 1974*

DAN FLAVIN

I went to Venice for the Biennale in 1970, and Flavin was one of the American artists in the exhibition. He wasn't at the gallery, but I went to the room where the Italian electrician was installing Flavin's piece and started to make a few photographs. "You know," the electrician told me, "I think Americans are very strange. This one wants to put a neon bulb in every corner, but he would get the same effect if he put a big one right in the middle." I didn't want to embarrass him, but I told him it was a work of art. He said, "That's all? If they asked me, I could make a woman out of neon."

Flavin is quiet and reserved. I photographed another installation of his work in New York, and I never even saw him touch the piece until the end of the day, when he went over and slightly twisted one of the bulbs.

Opposite page: *Leo Castelli Gallery, New York, 1970*

Leo Castelli Gallery, New York, 1970

Leo Castelli Gallery, New York, 1970; pages 98–99:
Leo Castelli Gallery, New York 1970

DUANE HANSON

After the Conceptual artists the magazines were hungry for pictures that had color and excitement. That's why I think the Realists and Photorealists got so popular. Art was very monastic and rigid, then all of a sudden there were New York storefronts and cars. Hanson's art seemed very ironic to me, with the same irony Oldenburg applied to his Pop objects, but especially successful because the people could recognize themselves in his figures without seeing what we see when we look at them. They are very popular in Europe because that is what Europeans think Americans look like—tourists in Miami with Bermuda shorts and cameras. To a European this is real Americana.

Opposite page: *With Ivan Karp, O.K. Harris Gallery, New York, 1972*

New York, 1972

New York, 1972

KEITH HARING

My daughter likes Keith Haring, and that's a good sign. For
a long time art was gray and detached. Artists seemed to think
they had to suffer— go into the desert without any water
and walk when the car broke down. I think they thought they
had to be heroes, maybe because they didn't fight in any wars.
But with Keith and the other young artists, art is fun again.
He is the Andy Warhol of the 1980s.

New York, 1985; pages 106–7: *The Palladium, New York, 1985*

MICHAEL HEIZER

After a day on the Nevada desert, where Mike was making his
motorcycle piece and I was photographing him, we went to
the casinos in Las Vegas. In just a little while I had won about
three or four hundred dollars, which was quite a lot in 1970.
Mike said, "Let's try putting our money together. Maybe we'll
hit it big." Well, we lost not only the money I had won, but
everything else besides. Without even enough for a taxi, we
had to walk miles back to the motel in the middle of the night,
and the next day we had to have his gallery wire us cash to
pay our bills. I always believed in Mike as an artist, but I never
went gambling with him again.

Mike loves the desert for its toughness and its beauty. I like
it too, but I am not so fond of hardship. He owns a house in
a place called Garden Valley, and his is the only private land
in the middle of an arms testing ground for the American
government. He is surrounded by missiles, and I think he
likes the idea of that kind of danger.

Opposite page: *Jean, Dry Lake, Nevada, 1970;* pages 110–11: *Mormon
Mesa, Nevada, 1970*

Jean Dry Lake, Nevada, 1970; opposite
page and pages 114–15: *Jean Dry Lake,
Nevada, 1970;* pages 116–17: *Garden
Valley, Nevada, 1974;* pages 118–19:
Silver Spring, Nevada, 1970

JASPER JOHNS

When I went to meet Jasper Johns at his studio in a former bank on the Bowery, I had to wait outside a few moments with the bums and the bottles and the trash. Then the doors swung open onto a huge room painted white with a big dome. There was soft music from the stereo, and Johns himself appeared dressed all in white. It was like leaving the Inferno and walking into heaven.

That day Johns was not painting but drawing. Drawing is hard to photograph, and Johns was not relaxed with the camera. He would work a few minutes, then look up to see what I was doing. That was the moment I waited for.

Opposite page: *New York, 1970*

Gemini, Los Angeles, 1977; opposite page: *New York, 1970*

Whitney Museum of American Art, New York, 1977;
opposite page: *New York 1970*

DONALD JUDD

When I visited him, Donald Judd was about to move out of
New York to the new studio he had built in Texas. He agreed to
see me one afternoon before he left, but it was on a day he was
not working. So instead of showing me how he worked, he took
me on a tour of his building. It was funny to me, coming from
Europe, to see so much space with just one or two pieces of
furniture in it. On one floor was a bedroom with just one bed
in it. On the next floor was a kid's room, then another floor
with a kitchen, then his office, and then the studio, and in the
basement a storage room. But since Judd's work is more a
product of mental activity rather than physical effort, it made
sense to photograph him in his surroundings.

Opposite page: *New York, 1970;* pages 128–29, 130–31: *New York, 1970*

ELLSWORTH KELLY

On the telephone artists always say they are very busy; they can only spend a few minutes with you. Then when you get there and they see you and talk to you, they seem to have a lot of time. They suggest things, ideas for photographs, places to go. That was how it was with Ellsworth Kelly. I went up to the Hudson River town where he lives to take a few photographs, and we spent the whole day driving around the countryside looking at barns.

Opposite page: *Chatham, New York, 1974*

Chatham, New York, 1974

Chatham, New York, 1974; pages 133–37: *Chatham, New York, 1974*

Chatham, New York, 1974; opposite page and pages 140–41:
Chatham, New York, 1974

ALFRED LESLIE

I met Alfred Leslie at the Whitney Museum of American Art,
when he was installing his painting *The Assassination of
Frank O'Hara*. He said I could take his picture, but we didn't
get together until several months later, when his dealer,
Richard Bellamy, called me up and asked if I would like to
go out to visit the Leslies in Amherst.

It was winter, very cold, with a lot of snow on the ground, so
we spent all day in the house talking and drinking. I was
fascinated by the picture of his pregnant wife. He had spent
months painting it, and by the time I arrived the baby had
been born. I thought it would be funny to show him with the
baby in front of the portrait—the sequel to the painting.

Opposite page: *Whitney Museum of American Art, New York, 1973*

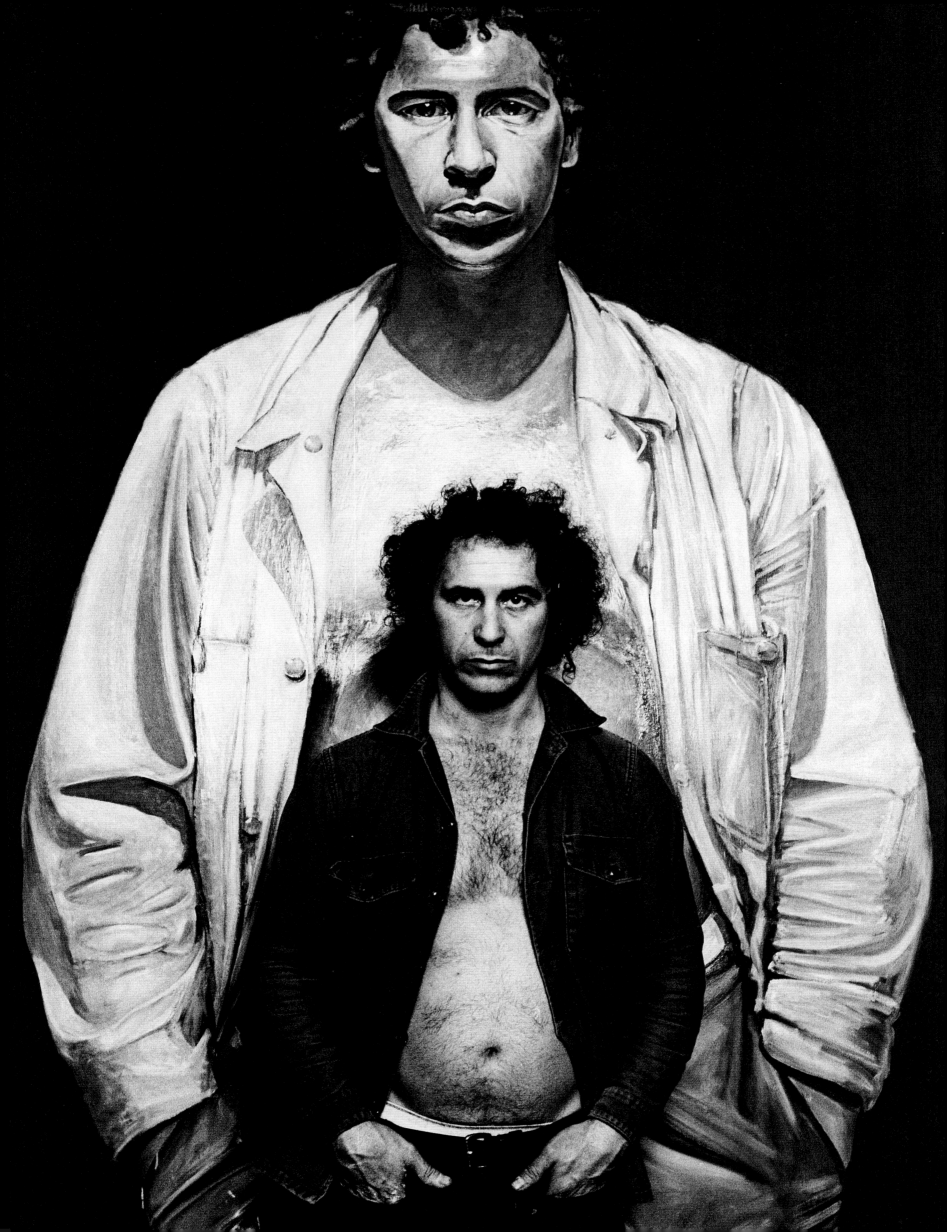

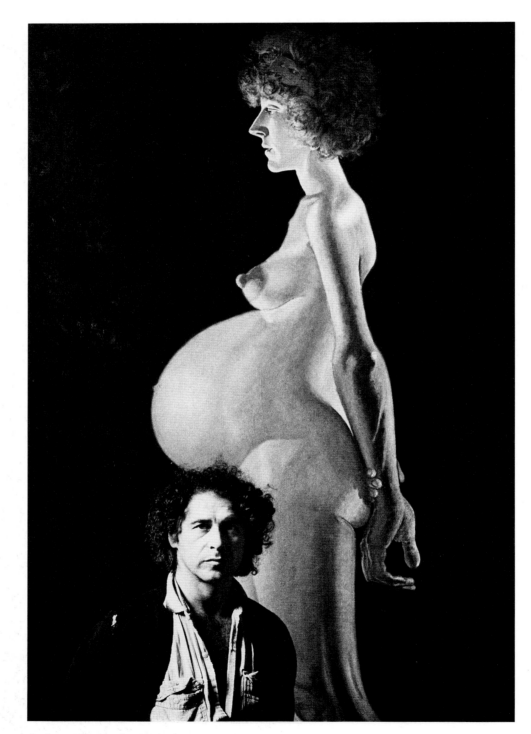

Amherst, Massachusetts, 1972

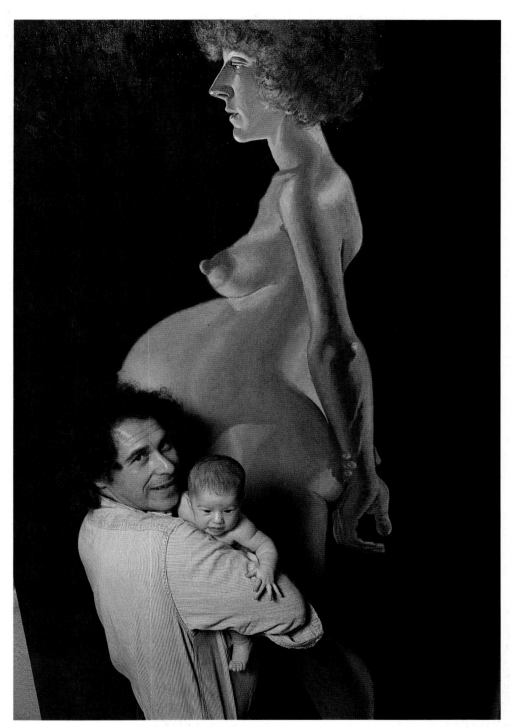

Amherst, Massachusetts, 1972; pages 146–47:
Whitney Museum of American Art, 1973

SOL LEWITT

By the time I met him in 1970, Sol Lewitt was already a well-established artist, so I was surprised by his place on Hester Street. He lived in an almost tenement kind of building, with bars on the windows. His little loft was organized but full of things, as if he had been collecting them all of his life. There was art by Carl Andre, Robert Smithson, and Eva Hesse, and artist's materials and tools, but what fascinated me was a piece of paper next to his drawing table that he uses for cleaning his pen. It was a piece in itself, an unselfconscious record of a month's work—the opposite of his drawings but just as obsessive.

New York, 1971

New York, 1970

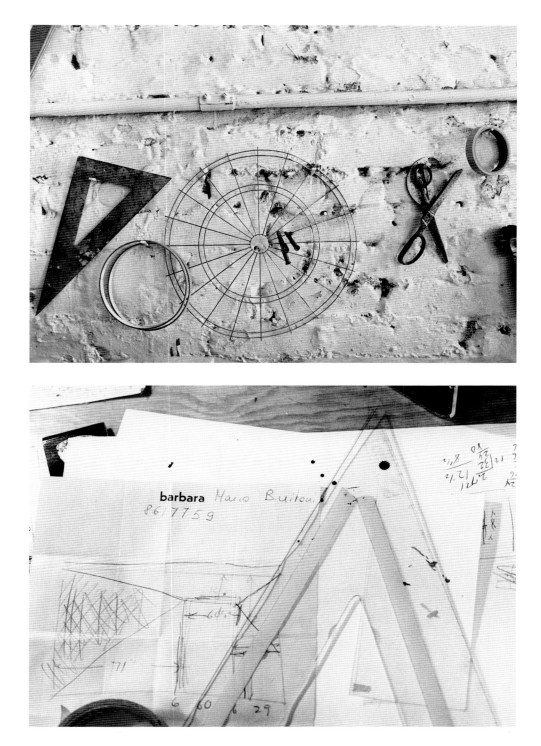

New York, 1970; pages 152–53: *New York, 1970*

Gemeentemuseum, The Hague, Netherlands, 1970

Gemeentemuseum, The Hague, Netherlands, 1970; pages
156–57: *Gemeentemuseum, The Hcgue, Netherlands, 1970*

ALEXANDER LIBERMAN

I called upon Alexander Liberman because I wanted to
interview him about photography for a film I was working on,
but while I was with him in his New York office, he couldn't
resist showing me some of his own sculpture projects. I was
very moved by the drawings, and in the end he invited me
to visit him in the Connecticut countryside the next weekend.
He sent a limousine down to New York to pick me up, and I
spent the day watching him work. I was surprised to see how
many things in his life are still Russian. He and his wife spoke
Russian to each other; we had a Russian soup for lunch; and
the yard was lined with birches, which I think of as
Russian trees.

Opposite page: *Warren, Connecticut, 1979;* pages 160–61: *Warren,
Connecticut, 1979*

ROY LICHTENSTEIN

Roy Lichtenstein always seemed to be completely available for photographs whenever I visited him. He never said no to anything, but he never stopped working either. He was busy on two, sometimes three paintings at a time.

One weekend in 1973 I went out and stayed in his house in the Hamptons on Long Island. What made the trip memorable to me is that Roy and I went to the drive-in together to see *Planet of the Apes*. As a teenager in Italy I had heard about drive-ins and dreamed of the time I might visit one with a girlfriend. Instead my first trip was with a Pop artist—not romantic, but somehow just as American.

Thanks to Roy I also attended my first presidential inauguration—Jimmy Carter's in 1977. He had an invitation to the ceremony, and I didn't, but as he started to go inside I asked him to hold his coat open. I crouched down behind it; the Secret Service didn't see me; and I sneaked into the White House.

Leo Castelli Gallery, New York, 1974

Southampton, 1973; pages 172–73: *Southampton, 1973*

AGNES MARTIN

A magazine sent me out to photograph Agnes Martin in New
Mexico, where she was building a house on a mesa near a
small town called Cuba. She picked me up in a car at the
Albuquerque airport, but when we got to Cuba, she changed
into overalls and boots, and we climbed into a jeep for the trip
up the mesa. Halfway there we were stopped by a landslide
that had covered the road, and she jumped out of the jeep and
grabbed a shovel. I grabbed another one. When we had cleared
the road and were back in the jeep, she said, "Well, at least
they didn't send me another weakling."

I had seen her paintings in New York, but on the mesa she
wasn't working on art; she was making bricks and chopping
wood. There was no one else around for miles, and one time I
tried to talk about it. "You have no electricity, no phone, no
neighbors," I said. "What happens if you get sick?" "I never
get sick," she said.

Opposite page: *Cuba, New Mexico, 1979*

Cuba, New Mexico, 1974

Cuba, New Mexico, 1974

Cuba, New Mexico, 1974

Cuba, New Mexico, 1974

Cuba, New Mexico, 1974

Cuba, New Mexico, 1974; pages 182–83: *Cuba, New Mexico, 1974*

ROBERT MORRIS

I started to photograph Robert Morris as he was making an installation at the Whitney Museum of American Art in April 1970. The piece he and his assistants were putting together was made of gigantic slabs of steel that took two cranes to lift them. One day one of the cranes folded over right in two, and the whole museum trembled. Fortunately the wheels of the crane kept the piece of steel from crushing one of the worker's legs, but everyone was white, including me. These things happen; it was nobody's fault, but everyone was shook up. The guards came running; the police arrived. Morris leaned his head against the side of the sculpture and just kept it there for about five minutes.

Whitney Museum of American Art, New York, 1970

Whitney Museum of American Art, New York, 1970

Whitney Museum of American Art, New York, 1970; pages
188–89: *Whitney Museum of American Art, New York, 1970*

Whitney Museum of American Art, New York, 1970

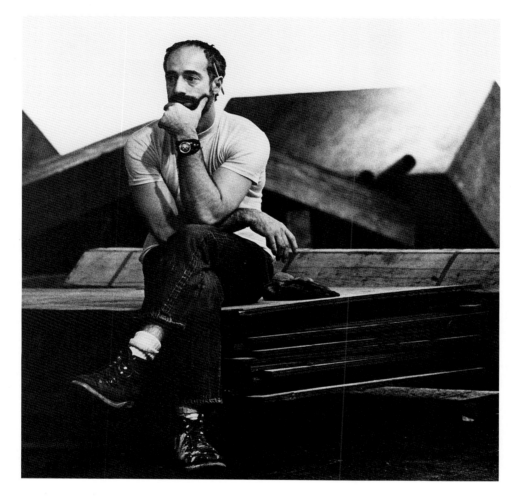

Whitney Museum of American Art,
New York, 1970; pages 192–93: *Whitney*
Museum of American Art, New York,
1970

BRUCE NAUMAN

He was sitting by the window, and while I was photographing
I noticed the shadow. Knowing his work, I moved until the
shadow divided his face in two.

Pasadena, California, 1970

San Jose, California, 1970; opposite page:
San Jose, California, 1970

San Jose, California, 1970; opposite page:
San Jose, California, 1970

Pasadena, California, 1970; opposite
page and pages 202–3: *San Jose,*
California, 1970

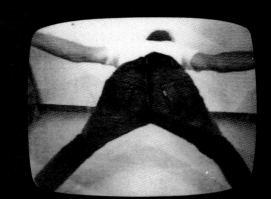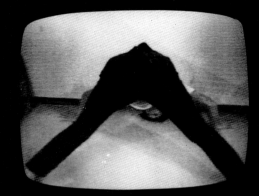
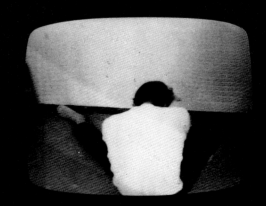
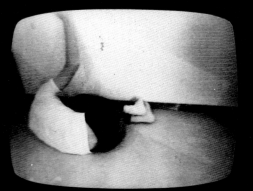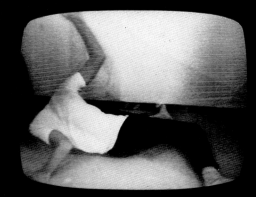

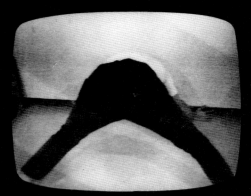 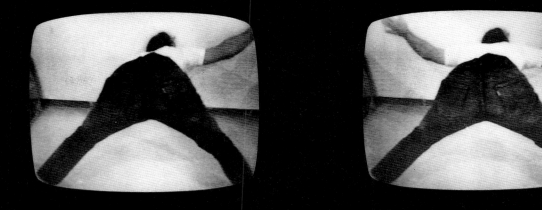 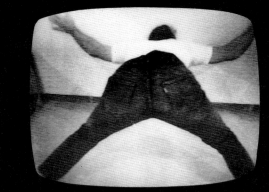

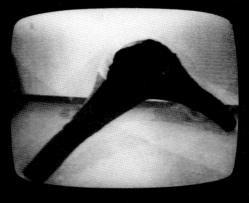 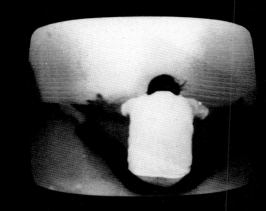 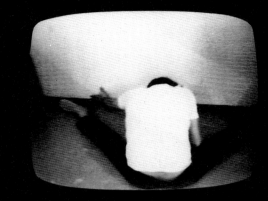

 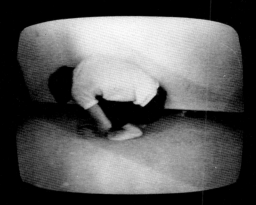 

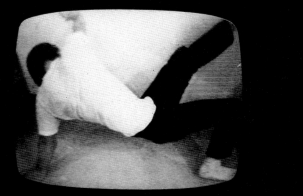 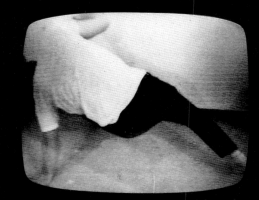 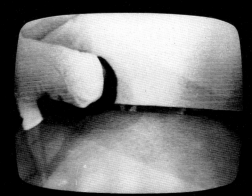

GEORGIA O'KEEFFE

After I had photographed Agnes Martin, I drove to Abiquiu,
New Mexico, to try to photograph Georgia O'Keeffe. I had
heard she was difficult to get to see, but I went to her house,
and she opened the door and invited me in. She was friendly,
but she said she didn't like having her picture taken. I said
that was all right; it was enough just to have met her.

We talked a while, and then she asked me to stay to lunch.
Afterwards I said I would really like to see her studio, and she
offered to show it to me. I didn't expect that I would be taking
any photographs, but as we went out the door she looked at me
and smiled. "Don't you want to take your camera?" she said.

Opposite page: *Abiquiu, New Mexico, 1974*

Abiquiu, New Mexico, 1974

Abiquiu, New Mexico, 1974

Abiquiu, New Mexico, 1974; opposite page and
pages 210–11, 212–13: *Abiquiu, New Mexico, 1974*

CLAES OLDENBURG

Pop Art is really Oldenburg to me. When I was doing a film
on Pop Art for Italian TV in 1978 I asked people on the streets
in Milan "What is Pop Art?" The best answer was from a guy
who was selling those kitsch plastic religious figures on
the sidewalk. A flatbed truck came down the street, carrying
a Fiat in a giant clear plastic box tied with a big bow. "That's
it," he said. "That's Pop." It's the size of Oldenburg's work
that makes them Pop, to me, not just their craziness.

When I photographed the mouse sculpture in Rhode Island,
I wanted to use people to give a sense of scale, but I was alone
and nobody ever came by. Then I decided it would look great
covered in birds. I bought about twenty pounds of fish, and I
started to throw them in the air. A few gulls flew in, then more
and more, but by the time enough had arrived, I had run out
of fish. I had one more shot in the camera when I noticed
the two figures standing there. At first I thought they were
nurses, but I found out they were nuns, which was even better
than seagulls.

Oldenburg likes to clown a lot, but I have seen him looking
serious. It was at the Macy's Thanksgiving Day parade
one year. Just as the big balloon of Mickey Mouse came past,
I looked into the crowd, and there was Oldenburg, all by
himself, staring up at this balloon that could have been one
of his sculptures.

New York, 1975

Leo Castelli Gallery, New York, 1975

Leo Castelli Gallery, New York, 1975;
pages 218–19: *New York, 1975*
pages 220–21: *Newport, Rhode Island, 1975*

MIMMO PALADINO

In the summer of 1984 I went to a small town near Abruzzo
to see Mimmo Paladino at his beautiful studio in a grove of
olive trees. He had been getting ready for a show of his work,
and his studio was full of finished paintings, but he wasn't
working. I suggested it would be great if he made a mask like
the faces in his pictures. So we went into the olive grove and
gathered sticks. Then he made cutouts from wood, mixed paint
with wax, and nailed on the sticks for horns.

The next day we went to the Roman town of Saepinum,
looking for the right mythical spot for the photograph.
There was a festival going on, and the townspeople had strung
colored lights along the old columns, so we had to
search for a corner with an ominous mood.

When I returned to New York I got a letter from Paladino. He
thanked me for the contact sheets I had sent him and wrote
that, since I had the idea for the mask, he wanted to send it to
me. Sure enough, a few weeks later, a big wooden crate arrived.

Saepinum, Italy, 1984

Saepinum, Italy, 1984

Saepinum, Italy, 1984; pages 226–27: *Saepinum, Italy, 1984*

ROBERT RAUSCHENBERG

Bob Rauschenberg was the first artist I met when I came to New York. It was spring 1969, and I was walking around Greenwich Village. I had seen photographs of Rauschenberg, so when a group of people came toward me, laughing and talking, I recognized the man in the middle as Rauschenberg. He was a famous artist and I was a twenty-seven-year-old photographer from Italy, but I got a little courage, and I spoke to him. Not only did he say that I could take his picture, but when I asked when, he said, "Come with us now. We're on our way to a party."

Opposite page: *New York, 1969*

National Gallery of Art, Washington, D.C., 1976

National Gallery of Art, Washington, D.C., 1976

National Gallery of Art, Washington, D.C., 1976

National Gallery of Art, Washington, D.C., 1976: pages 234–
35: *New York, 1970;* pages 236–37: *Hamedabad, India, 1975*

JAMES ROSENQUIST

I met Jim Rosenquist through a common friend, Claude
Picasso. We went to Jim's studio on Wooster Street, and the
lasting impression I have is of the confusion of his loft: paint,
paperclips, brushes, photographs, luggage, beach umbrellas, a
huge mountain of Styrofoam, clothes, books, and barbed wire
filled the space. But Jim seemed completely comfortable, and
when he needed something he knew exactly where to find it.

I visited Jim during the years in many studios, and they all
have one thing in common: chaos. Maybe it is an important
part of his work.

Of all of the so-called Pop artists, Jim is the one I am closest
to. One December I was at home as the doorbell rang. I went
downstairs and opened the door, and there was Jim. He gave
me a hug and a huge Italian prosciutto ham. "Happy Birthday,"
he said, and disappeared into the night.

Opposite page and pages 240–41, 242–43: *Aripeka, Florida, 1985*

DAVID SALLE

It took me a long time to get around to taking David Salle's picture. When I first met him he said he liked cigars. I was on my way to Cuba the next week, so I said I'd bring him some. When I got back he had gone to Switzerland, and by the time he got back from Switzerland I had finished the cigars.

New York, 1983; pages 246–47: *New York, 1983*

KENNY SCHARF

When I photographed Kenny he was painting a picture that
eventually went to the Whitney Museum of American Art.
Kenny went to Paris, and he never knew what happened to the
pictures. A French magazine published some of them, and
one day he happened to buy a copy and opened it by accident
to a double-page spread of his work. That was the first thing
he told me when he saw me again.

Opposite page: *The Palladium, New York, 1985;* pages 250–51: *Tony
Shafrazi Gallery, New York, 1984*

JULIAN SCHNABEL

When I called he said, "I'm on my way out to Long Island, but why don't you come along." I took my daughter, Maya, who was three years old, and we had a very nice time.

In the morning I was walking around the house, and I saw under it broken vases, horns, bones, and the kind of canvas you use to cover a boat. I said, "Why don't you make something out of this?" We carried the canvas out to the beach, and Julian started to make a painting. As the day wore on, more and more people started to walk by. One old lady came over, and she said, "What's it supposed to be?"

Julian said, "It's a painting."

"Where can we see it?"

"At the Museum of Modern Art," he said.

Opposite page and pages 254–55: *Amagansett, Long Island, 1982*

Amagansett, Long Island, 1982

Amagansett, Long Island, 1982; pages 258–59:
Amagansett, Long Island, 1982

RICHARD SERRA

I was at Jasper Johns's studio taking his picture, and a guy came in and started heating up lead and throwing it in the corner. Jasper said he was Richard Serra and that he was making a sculpture.

For me Serra was one of the most surprising artists of the 1970s. I had been photographing traditional painters and sculptors, and Serra's way of working was completely new to me. Meeting him gave me the idea for putting together the artists in the *New Avant-Garde*.

Opposite page: *New York, 1970*

Los Angeles, 1974; opposite page: *Los Angeles, 1974*

Leo Castelli Gallery, New York, 1981

Leo Castelli Gallery, New York, 1981; pages 266–67:
Leo Castelli Gallery, New York, 1981

ROBERT SMITHSON

We were in Utah, in a small town, where Bob was making
the *Spiral Jetty* out on the salt flats. Bob was pretty strange
looking, always in black; I had long hair; I looked like an
Indian; and all of us were pretty dirty. We went to a famous
steak house for dinner. The organ was playing, and all the
women were in dresses with puffed sleeves like dolls. It was
noisy in there, but when we came in the door, the organ
stopped, and nobody spoke. The dead silence continued for a
minute or so, then slowly the organist began to pick out a
few notes, then a few chords, then the talking began, and there
was life again.

In 1973 Smithson died when the small plane he was in crashed
on the site of his *Amarillo Ramp*. There were three people in
the plane, and one of them was a photographer. Right after
that *Artforum* sent me down to take pictures of the *Ramp*.
There were still parts of the airplane lying on the ground. I
took a look, and I realized you couldn't really photograph a
piece that size from the ground; you had to have an aerial view.
They looked at me funny when I said I wanted to go up, but I
said, "This piece already took the lives of three people. It isn't
going to get me."

Great Salt Lake, Utah, 1970

Great Salt Lake, Utah, 1970

Great Salt Lake, Utah, 1970; pages 272–73: *Great Salt Lake, Utah, 1970*

Great Salt Lake, Utah, 1970; opposite
page and pages 276–77, 278–79:
Great Salt Lake, Utah, 1970

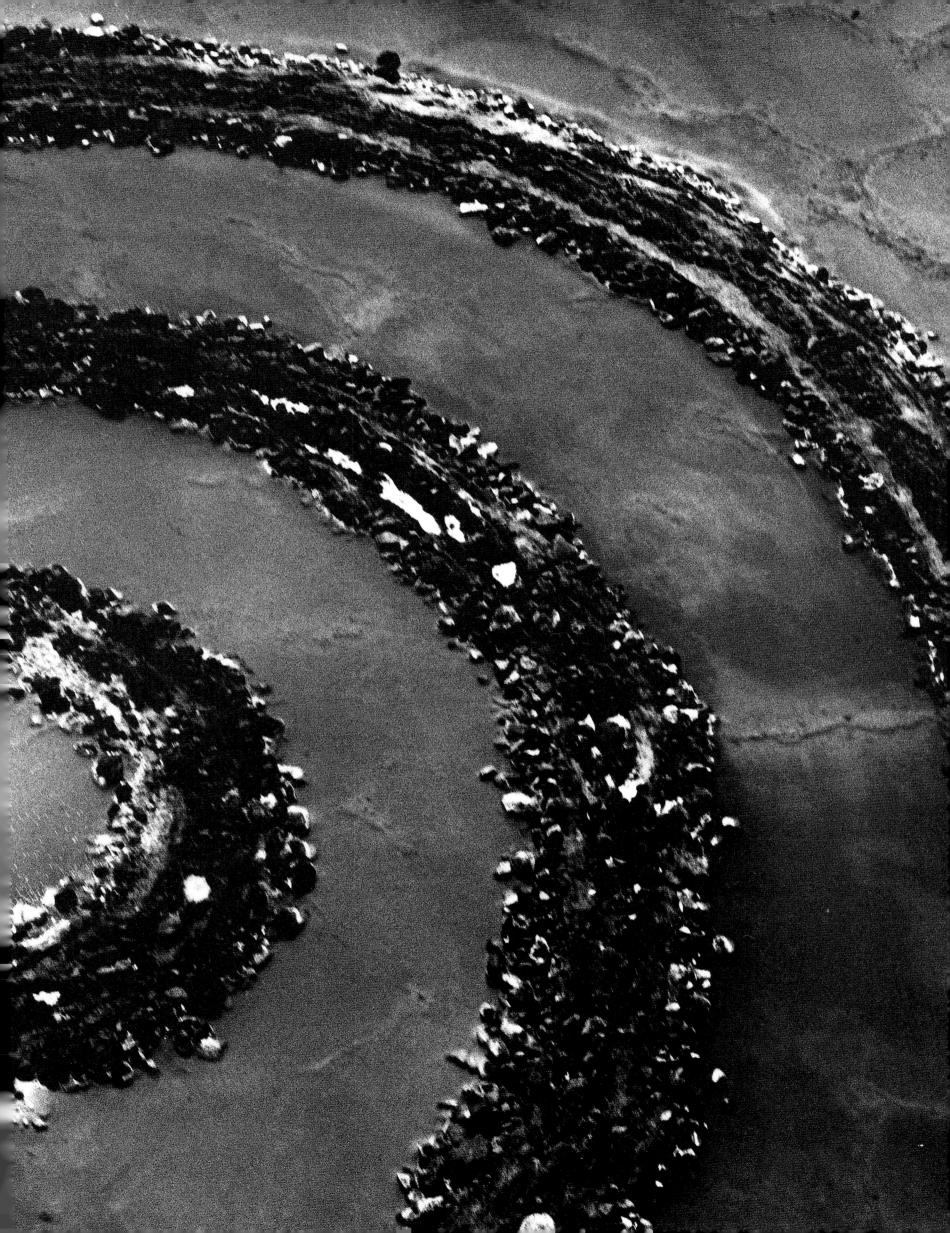

FRANK STELLA

Stella was one of the big names in art when I arrived in New York, and I always wanted to photograph him. When I finally got the chance I was very excited. I wanted to ask him if he was Italian and a lot of other things. When I got to his studio I introduced myself, and he said "Hi." That was the last word he said until I was on my way out, and I said, "I'm going now," and he said, "Oh. Goodbye." He wasn't unfriendly, I think. He was just concentrating on his painting so hard he wasn't really conscious I was there.

New York, 1981; pages 282–83: *New York, 1970*

CLYFFORD STILL

A lot of people had told me it was impossible to photograph
Still, that he was camera-shy. But I found out that he was
having an exhibition at the Metropolitan Museum of Art, so I
went over there, and without asking anybody walked past the
guards into the gallery where they were hanging the paintings.
I started to take pictures from a distance, moving closer to
Still a few steps at a time. After a while I knew that he had
seen me and he hadn't said anything, so I walked right up
to him and said I wanted to take his picture. He just turned
around and posed.

Opposite page and pages 286–87: *The Metropolitan Museum of Art,
New York, 1978*

ANDY WARHOL

Andy Warhol is kind of an embarrassing subject for a
photographer. He is so open he never says no to having his
picture taken, and he will do anything you ask him to; you
can move him around like a doll. After a while I wanted him
to resist, to create tension. I wanted to photograph something
real from his own life—that's why I told him to lie down on
the bed.

Opposite page: *New York, 1972;* pages 290–91: *Corcoran Gallery of Art,
Washington, D.C., 1977;* pages 292–93: *Whitney Museum of American Art,
New York, 1971*

New York, 1969; opposite page: *New York, 1975*

New York, 1971; opposite page: *New York, 1971;* pages 298–99:
With Giorgio de Chirico, New York, 1972

Biographies

Carl Andre (b. 1935)
In New York in the mid-1960s, Carl Andre became a prominent Minimal artist. His sculptures led him to Conceptual artworks—blocks of wood, piles of bricks, and metal slabs in checkerboard configurations—in which the objects themselves were less important than their arrangements in the environment. Each "temporary" work transforms its location, incorporating a sense of place into the idea of art.

Joseph Beuys (b. 1921)
The German artist Joseph Beuys derives much of his art from emotional experiences in his past—memories of his childhood and of his days as a fighter pilot in World War II. As a Conceptual artist, he has earned an international reputation for his performances, which are often political in content, and for his sculptural assemblages, made of such organic materials as sheep fat and wax. A survey of Beuys's work was held at the Solomon R. Guggenheim Museum in 1979. Beuys lives in Düsseldorf, West Germany.

Jonathan Borofsky (b. 1942)
Working in a variety of media, Jonathan Borofsky creates his works mostly from figures—both human and numeric. His monumental black two-dimensional men with hammers complement similar creatures painted on gallery walls and smaller drawings of numbers. A traveling exhibition of his work toured several major museums in the United States in 1984–85. Borofsky lives in Venice, California.

Sandro Chia (b. 1946)
One of the major Italian Neoexpressionist painters to emerge in the last decade, Sandro Chia paints large figures with round faces that resemble characters from classical art and literature in the heroic or bucolic tradition. He was born in Florence, and now lives in Italy and New York.

Christo (Christo Javacheff; b. 1935)
Christo was born in Bulgaria, moved to Paris in 1958, and settled in New York in 1964. Since then he has become known to the art world and to the general public for his environmental projects. He has wrapped buildings, a length of the Australian coastline, and several islands off the coast of Florida in plastic, and erected the *Running Fence,* which zigzagged across twenty-four miles of California countryside. His works have attracted attention and often controversy.

Francesco Clemente (b. 1952)
Identified with the group of Italian Neoexpressionist painters, Francesco Clemente lives and works in Italy and in Madras, India. Both places have influenced his vivid style and his subject matter of figures, self-portraits, and haunting symbolic images.

Chuck Close (b. 1940)
The large, realistic portraits by Chuck Close appear at first to be oversized photographic images—close-up frontal views of faces. But whether his medium is pastel, charcoal, or acrylic, Close creates his portraits in a painstaking, stroke-by-stroke technique, most recently using his thumbprint to build his monumental realist works. Close lives in New York.

Enzo Cucchi (b. 1950)
Enzo Cucchi, one of the leading Neoexpressionist artists to emerge in the late 1970s, lives and works in Ancona, Italy. His paintings are often mythological inventions, incorporating classical references and symbols with other elements—skulls, faces, and roosters, for example—in dark imaginary landscapes.

Willem de Kooning (b. 1904)
Since the 1940s, Willem de Kooning has been acknowledged to be one of America's leading Abstract Expressionist painters, best known for his female nudes in vivid colors. De Kooning emigrated from the Netherlands to the United States in 1926, spent many years in New York City, and now lives in East Hampton, Long Island.

Walter De Maria (b. 1935)
In the 1970s Walter De Maria became a leading figure among Minimal and land artists. His many projects include an "earth room" for a New York gallery in 1977, and the *Broken Kilometer,* an environmental work presented in New York in 1979. Pushing the Minimal notion to its limits, De Maria sometimes uses chance as a means of depersonalizing and objectifying the creation of a work of art.

Mark di Suvero (b. 1933)
Mark di Suvero is a sculptor who makes large abstract works of metal and wood using straight lines and rectilinear forms. He was born in Shanghai, studied art at the University of California, spent several years in Europe during the 1970s, and now lives in New York, where he exhibits at Richard Bellamy's Oil and Steel Gallery.

Dan Flavin (b. 1933)
The sculptures of Dan Flavin are arrangements of fluorescent tubes in different hues that fill a space with color and light. The Minimal works, which are planned by Flavin and installed by technicians at the site, are tailored to their individual environment.

Duane Hanson (b. 1925)
Duane Hanson's life-sized figures have an eerie verisimilitude. Hanson chooses "ordinary" people for many of his works, such as policemen and tourists with Bermuda shorts and cameras.

Keith Haring (b. 1958)
Breaking into the galleries from the art scene of the street, Keith Haring is a phenomenon of the 1980s. His stylized graffiti drawings of babies, dancing figures, TV screens, and other elements of popular culture have appeared on subway as well as museum walls.

Michael Heizer (b. 1944)
Primarily known as a maker of earthworks in the deserts of the West, Heizer has also made smaller sculptures and paintings. Among his most ambitious undertakings is the moving of some 40,000 tons of earth by carving and shaping. He has also used his motorcycle to etch circles in the desert surface, producing a temporary work visible only from the air.

Jasper Johns (b. 1930)
Along with Robert Rauschenberg, Jasper Johns contributed to the transition in American painting from Abstract Expressionism, which dominated avant-garde art of the 1940s and 1950s, to Pop Art, which emerged in the early 1960s. His early paintings of targets and American flags not only treated recognizable popular objects as their subject matter, but also called attention to the indisputable two-dimensionality of painting itself. Johns lives and works in New York. A retrospective of his painting and graphic art was held at the Whitney Museum of American Art in 1977.

Donald Judd (b. 1928)
Donald Judd has continued in the Minimal art tradition that brought him to prominence in the late 1960s. His spare sculptures are composed primarily of separate geometric elements—usually boxes—in such materials as concrete, polished steel, and painted wood.

Ellsworth Kelly (b. 1923)
Ellsworth Kelly's paintings, drawings, and graphic works are based on such organic forms as leaf shapes, simply and elegantly rendered. Sometimes considered a "hard-edge" abstractionist and Minimal artist, Kelly has a unique approach to form and color that makes him difficult to categorize with any group. Kelly lives in Chatham, New York.

Alfred Leslie (b. 1927)
Alfred Leslie began his career as an "action painter" in the 1940s and 1950s, freely distributing paint on large canvases. In 1964 he turned to realistic painting, wanting to acknowledge that the pre-abstract tradition had validity. He has executed many large portraits and has also rendered biblical and other narrative themes in monumental heroic paintings.

Sol Lewitt (b. 1928)
Through geometric sculptures and rigidly repetitive line drawings, Sol Lewitt has become known as one of the principal figures of the Conceptual Art movement. Lewitt lives in New York, where he has collaborated with dancer Lucinda Childs and composer Philip Glass on performances.

Alexander Liberman (b. 1912)
Both a painter and a sculptor, Alexander Liberman uses geometric forms as the basic elements of his compositions. He studied in Paris as a youth, and today lives in New York and Connecticut. Many of his large painted-steel sculptures have been installed in public spaces and sculpture parks.

Roy Lichtenstein (b. 1923)
Beginning in the mid-1960s Roy Lichtenstein became identified with the Pop Art movement. His blown-up images of advertisements and comic-strip soldiers made use of the newspaper Benday dot, heavy outlines, and primary colors. These stylistic features have since been incorporated into increasingly sophisticated treatments of art's classics—from van Gogh to Picasso, from modern sculpture to the landscape tradition. Lichtenstein lives in New York.

Agnes Martin (b. 1912)
Agnes Martin has been painting since the 1940s, evolving through a phase of biomorphic abstraction to her present delicate grid paintings. Born in Saskatchewan, Canada, she now lives in New Mexico. Her move to the Southwest in 1967 signaled the current direction of her painting style—pale tonalities borrowed from the landscape in a linear framework.

Robert Morris (b. 1931)
Since the 1960s, Robert Morris has been involved with experiments that stretch the traditional limits of three-dimensional art. Early pieces incorporated tape recordings and mirrored cubes. Recent work includes mirrors in large, colorful sculptural frames. During the 1960s, working in New York, Morris participated in dance and theater performances, and made Minimal sculptures, some composed of large pieces of steel and concrete.

Bruce Nauman (b. 1941)
A multimedia artist, Bruce Nauman has worked with films, photographs, videotapes, light systems, and a variety of plastic materials. His work is self-reflective; he used his own body as a mold for works produced in the mid-1960s, and his image has been the predominant feature of some of his video performances.

Georgia O'Keeffe (b. 1887)
Georgia O'Keeffe's highly individual style can be seen even in her earliest drawings, of about 1915. She is considered one of the earliest American modernist painters. She had her first exhibition at the photographer Alfred Stieglitz's "291" Gallery in 1916, and later married him. Stieglitz died in 1947, and in 1949 O'Keeffe moved to Abiquiu, New Mexico, where she still lives today. From skyscrapers in New York to iris blossoms to New Mexican sunsets, O'Keeffe renders her subjects with directness and intensity.

Claes Oldenburg (b. 1929)
The Pop Art movement brought Claes Oldenburg to the forefront of the American art scene. After staging such environments as the *Street* and the *Store,* Oldenburg created giant soft sculptures of hamburgers, pay telephones, fans, and other icons of popular culture. Applying the oversize concept to the theme of monuments, he made a series of proposals for public works, including a toilet-tank mechanism for the Thames River and the controversial lipstick tube installed at Yale University. Oldenburg is also widely respected as a draftsman.

Mimmo Paladino (b. 1948)
In Mimmo Paladino's expressive paintings there is always a note of darkness. His themes are symbolic and mythological, dealing with primordial concepts of life and death. Paladino lives in Italy and exhibits internationally. His paintings were shown at the Sperone-Westwater Gallery in New York in 1985.

Robert Rauschenberg (b. 1925)
Widely acknowledged as one of the most influential contemporary artists, Rauschenberg achieved international fame in 1964, when he became the first American to win the painting prize at the Venice Biennale since James Abbott McNeill Whistler. Since his combine paintings of the 1960s, which employed startling collage effects, Rauschenberg has experimented in nearly every medium open to the artist—from painting and graphic art to cardboard boxes. Rauschenberg divides his time between New York and Florida, when he is not traveling with his projects.

James Rosenquist (b. 1933)
James Rosenquist's career has seen active and quiescent periods, recently reaching a high point with a series of monumental paintings and a retrospective exhibition that opened at the Denver Art Museum in 1985. In the Pop era Rosenquist broke onto the scene with his dramatic billboard-inspired paintings that featured a mix of incongruous elements, such as figures juxtaposed against canned spaghetti. His new works are enormous still-lifes of the imagination, in which six-foot flowers may float next to a disembodied set of teeth.

David Salle (b. 1952)
Born in Oklahoma, Salle now lives in New York. He holds a Master of Fine Arts degree from the California Institute of the Arts. His paintings have a collage effect, combining female nudes, 1950s furniture, images from childhood memories, and stenciled words. These elements are rendered in often jarringly different styles, juxtaposing carefully detailed realism with gestural drawing.

Kenny Scharf (b. 1958)
Kenny Scharf is one of the new younger artists who began his career in the East Village galleries. His colorful paintings and environments are packed with humorous imagery in a sophisticated graffiti style. His fantastic installations include a dream closet at the Whitney Museum of American Art's Biennial Exhibition in 1985 and a lavatory in the Palladium nightclub.

Julian Schnabel (b. 1951)
One of the best-known and most controversial artists to emerge in the late 1970s, Julian Schnabel has been criticized for an overly commercial attitude and a style that borrows heavily from that of other artists. The most distinctive element in his collage-paintings is broken crockery, spread across the picture plane. Recent exhibitions of his work, include a retrospective at the Stedelijk Museum, Amsterdam, in 1982.

Richard Serra (b. 1939)
One of the features of Richard Serra's working method is an involvement with materials, whether molten lead or large steel plates, and with the process of creating art. Many of his pieces are so large that they transform the interior or exterior space in which they are installed. Serra lives in New York.

Robert Smithson (1938–1973)
Before his death in an airplane accident, Robert Smithson had become a prominent figure among Minimal artists working in the late 1960s and early 1970s. He organized and executed several large earthworks in the Southwest, including *Spiral Jetty* on the Great Salt Lake, Nevada (1970) and the piece on which he was working at the time of his death, *Amarillo Ramp.*

Frank Stella (b. 1936)
Frank Stella began his career in the 1950s with all-black paintings but soon moved into the brightly colored, hard-edged stripe paintings for which he became known in the 1960s. He has pursued many new directions since then, including unusually shaped canvases and more recent collages. Stella lives in New York.

Clyfford Still (1904–1980)
Clyfford Still was a major Abstract Expressionist. His large paintings usually feature one dominant color that saturates the canvas, fading and blurring at the edges. In 1979, just before his death, the Metropolitan Museum of Art in New York held a major retrospective exhibition of his paintings.

Andy Warhol (b. 1928)
Before becoming famous as an artist and as the man who predicted universal and short-lived fame for everyone in the future, Andy Warhol was a successful commercial artist and illustrator. In the early 1960s he began to paint Coca-Cola bottles and build wooden Brillo boxes, quickly becoming one of the most prominent Pop artists. His multiple images of famous personalities pointed out the mass production aspects of modern culture, which his works simultaneously celebrate and criticize. Warhol is also a filmmaker, whose credits include an eight-hour film of the Empire State Building and *Chelsea Girls.*